Determined to Live

How I Endured 48 Surgeries
Due to Gastric Bypass

LYNETTE R. GOODE

WESTBOW
PRESS
A DIVISION OF THOMAS NELSON

WestBow Press books may be ordered through booksellers or by contacting:

WestBow Press
A Division of Thomas Nelson
1663 Liberty Drive
Bloomington, IN 47403
www.westbowpress.com
1-(866) 928-1240

ISBN: 978-1-4497-8787-5 (sc)
ISBN: 978-1-4497-8786-8 (hc)
ISBN: 978-1-4497-8788-2 (e)

Library of Congress Control Number: 2013904868

Printed in the United States of America.

WestBow Press rev. date: 5/3/2013

MAR • 68

THE JOSEPH RUFFIN FAMILY. HELLO WORLD!

Table of Contents

*T*his book is dedicated to God and my wonderful husband Tyrone Leon Goode. I never would have thought that we would go through the things we have over the past sixteen years. Every time the doctor would tell you I was not going to make it, you made me believe that I would. When I was so weak and tired of fighting the battle, you would not allow me to give up. You are an example of what a husband and father does when things get really tough. We have been through so much with my family and your family, but we made it, honey. I will never forget that morning when you came to the hospital at 2:30 in the morning. I felt someone kissing me on my head, and it was you. Somehow you knew I was giving up because I was tired of fighting for my life. You made me promise that I would not give up, and I didn't because I am here to tell the story. People said we were not going to make it one year, but on July 8, 2013 we will be married for twenty-four years. I love you so much. The best is yet to come, honey. When God made you, he made you just for me and no one else.

ACKNOWLEDGMENTS

I would like to thank my parents for being so unselfish when I became very ill. You all literally rotated months to take care of my family. When I was growing up, you all encouraged all of us to give our best at whatever we did. Dad, before God called you home you got to see your baby girl graduate from college. You and Mom were so happy. There are no perfect parents, but you all did well by us. Dad, I know you are sitting in heaven just smiling saying that's my baby. Mom, I love you so much. As long as I live I will forever be looking out for you.

Tiffany, you are our one and only child. I want to thank you for editing my book. You could have been doing a lot of stuff because I was so sick most of your childhood life, but you didn't. When I sit back and look at the young woman you have become, I can give all the credit to God. You are an awesome young woman.

I was not there for most of your early childhood years, but I am here now, and we can do some damage control to your daddy's wallet. Every moment that we spend together is just so special to me. The world will know you all by yourself because you have so many gifts and talents that only God could have given to you.

Special gratitude to Angel Pope, when I asked you to type my manuscript because my hands would not allow me to type, you said yes. Thank you so much for listening to all those hours of tapes and putting it on paper. I will always be indebted to you. Special thanks to my best friend Lois Lane Parson for editing my book also. We will always be sisters.

Bishop Robert E. Williams, Sr., words cannot explain how much you have been there for me and my family. Through all the surgeries that I have had, you were there to comfort my family and pray for me before I went into the operating room. The relationship that you have with my family is just awesome. God put us under your leadership, and you are our spiritual head. Through all of the personal things that I went through at the hospital, you were right at the hospital with me. I will never forget that Sunday evening when you came to visit me in PICU. When the door opened at this time I could only see the colors of black and blue. He said, "Girl, I cannot have you in the hospital with your hands looking like that." Then he put lotion on my hands. That was so special to me. I want you to know Bishop; we have grown so much under your leadership. You have been a confidant to me over the years. There are certain things I have shared with only you and God.

I am so thankful for my team of doctors. Dr. Schroder, you know me better in the inside more than myself because you have done most of my surgeries except for a few. You always took the lead, and you never gave up on me. Dr. Coleman, thank you so much for allowing me to detox when you knew it was going to be an uphill battle because you could not use the drugs that you needed to because in the past they had messed with my heart. Dr. Gelrud, I will never forget you. We had to make some difficult decisions when it came to my stomach issues. You never gave up on me or my family. Dr. Call, I just want to say thank you for your funny personality and for believing in me the first time we met. Bill Payne, thank you for pushing me in physical therapy to be at the place I am at now. Dr. Sandra Bell, thank you so much for taking care of Tiffany for nineteen years and writing notes on what you had discussed with my husband. Dr. Kim Harris, Dr. Mary Wells, Dr. Maria Iouna, Dr. Joseph Evers, Dr. Neher, Dr. Lothe, and Dr. Richard Byrd, you all are the best. Dr. Palisano, you diagnosed an eye disease and put me on the right medication. You all are very special to me.

I am especially thankful to Brenda Simmons and Lawanda Bond for taking Tiffany to and from school and for making sure that she was participating in her extracurricular activities.

I want to thank all the staff in the operating room, dietary department, nursing staff, registration department, and house cleaning department at St. Mary's Hospital in Richmond, Virginia for taking such good care of me.

In gratitude I would like to thank Mom Carrie Woody Sayles. You would make sure that I needed anything when you got home from work. You are not with us anymore, but I will see you again. Ms. Sarah Elizabeth Johnson, you took care of Tiffany, and you would not charge us anything. Words can never express how grateful we were for you. You have gone on to be with the Lord also.

To my adopted grandmothers, Grandmother Sarah Celess Woody and Ms. Gladys J. Winston. Grandmother Gladys J. Winston, I just hope and pray when I am in my eighties I will be able to continue to live an independent life and not depend on anyone but God. Grandmother Sarah Celess Woody, you are in your nineties, and I get so excited and encouraged every day when I see you driving, shopping, and doing everything a young person would do. When I see you doing these things, it gives me the courage to keep fighting for my life. God answered my prayers. I have always wanted grandmothers like you. I just want to tell you both I love you so much.

God answered my prayers also when he gave me Juwarne Hughes and Gwen Johnson as big sisters. You both play different roles in my life, but each role is so important to me. I know sometimes I can be very difficult, but you all keep me in the right place I need to be. I can truly share that I trust you both with my life. I love you both so very much.

Rhonda Croston, words cannot explain how much you mean to me. When you first walked into my house the first thing that I was saying in my mind was this is another home health nurse I am going to fire. I am so thankful that I didn't because you have proven to be the best home health nurse I have ever had. Not only are you my best home health nurse, you are one of my best friends. Always remember I am thankful for you, I love you so much.

Reverend Frank L. Aikens, you married Leon and I. There has always been a bond between us. No one will ever know how many times you would come and counsel Leon and I when we first got married. You will always be my home church pastor. You helped save our marriage when we first got married.

Mr. Frank Thornton, when I was able to drive you gave me the opportunity to come and talk to your French class about eating healthy and about not using drugs. We have such an awesome friendship now. Thanks for giving me a chance. Mrs. Bonnie-Connor Gray, you allowed me to come and talk to the middle and high school students at different times. You also gave me a chance to be open about how it is so important to eat healthy and to stay away from drugs.

Special thanks to the Richmond International Raceway. You all believed in my vision when others did not. I will always be grateful to Jackie Frame, Doug Fritz, Dennis Bieckmeier and Richie Denzler.

Foy and Mary Shaw, you all took such good care of me when I was so sick. Mama Shaw, you gave me an outlet to help deal with my sickness. You taught me how to garden so well. Papa Shaw, you would come over to sit with me because all of my nursing staff would be gone. I love the both of you so much.

Rock, my faithful German Shepherd. You saved my life twice because my sugar dropped so low. My doctor told me that you licked me enough with the glucose in your salvia to penetrate my body so I could get something to drink to bring my sugar up.

Dr. James Cornelius, I have never met a teacher in college that has your teaching style. After taking all of your classes you have become someone that I just enjoy. I don't think you know how much I adore you. Each time we talk you are always encouraging me. You assure me that everything will be all right because God is the head of my life. Wherever you are, you will always have a special place in my heart

Finally, I would like to thank my church family for praying for me when I could not.

Thanks to the Westbury Café for having some healthy food that I could eat. You all are the best.

CHAPTER 1

Parents

There is one decision in life that we do not get to make, and that is what family we are born into. When I was growing up, our home was far from normal. I guess I did not realize that until I became older.

Both of my parents came from large, strict households. I'll talk about my father first. My father was the youngest male of his siblings. His younger sister was the baby girl. Their father, my grandfather, was very abusive. All the children called him Pa. Pa would make them work on the farm from sunup to sundown. Pa was abusive to all of his children except for one. I am not going to mention any names. I think in every family there is a favorite child; parents may not want to admit this, but it is true. They may say, "I love all my children the same," but it is impossible to do that because each child has a unique personality.

My father was not allowed to go to school. As a result, he was illiterate. He could not read or write, and he had no interest in learning. One day I was curious, so I asked my father if Grandpa was abusive to Grandma, and he told me no. He told me that the worst thing that he would do was curse at her from time to time. I told my father that is emotional abuse, which in my opinion is the worst kind of abuse. I asked my father what Grandma would do, and he told me that she would just keep singing her favorite hymn, "I'll Fly Away." When my dad told me that, I couldn't help myself—I just began to cry. My father was a very prideful man, and I could see that he really wanted to cry, but because of his pride, he wouldn't let a tear drop from his eyes. He just got up and walked away. I could see he was hurting. He was very close to his mother.

✳✳✳

Things finally reached a boiling point with my dad and his father. It was the Fourth of July, and Dad wanted to go to see the fireworks. Pa told him he could not go. My dad began talking back to Pa, so Pa went and got his shotgun and shot at my dad. The only way Dad could save himself was to jump over the fence. That was the last time my dad saw his father alive.

I never got the chance to meet Pa, because he died before I was born. If he was anything like my father said, I don't think I would have wanted to meet him. God works in mysterious ways, because I did get the chance to meet Grandma Francis, my dad's mother. When I first met her, I was nervous because I thought she was mean like her husband, but she was the most loving person that anyone would want to have as a grandmother. I regret that I was not able to spend more time with her. My aunts took my grandmother to North Carolina to care for her. I have often wondered what kind of circumstances led her to marry Pa, because they were complete opposites. My conclusion is that he did not show his aggressive side to her until after they were married and had children.

My father married twice. His first wife wasn't able to have children. It was rumored that he was abusive to her. They were married ten or more years, and then she died of cancer.

My father was the smartest person I have ever known, despite not having had any type of education. If he had gone to school, he probably could have been a mathematician. He could count money faster than anyone I have ever seen. He taught us multiplication at young ages. We could be riding down the highway, and he would look at the license plates of cars and say what state they were from. I asked him how he could do that, and he said he had a gift called "motherwith."

Just as my father had, my mother also came from a strict household, from what my mother has explained to me. Her mother made all of her children's clothes, which was not a lot. They did not have the money to buy clothes for so many children. Mom said that she had to wear shoes with holes in them to school. My mother quit school in the tenth grade. From what my mother told me, she dropped out at such a young age because grandmother needed her to stay at home because there were things that had to be done before she got home from work.

I do not remember my grandmother working two jobs. This was something that I had no idea about, until one of my mother's siblings told me. One thing that they always had was food because my grandfather always had a big garden with vegetables. He raised and killed hogs. The parts of the hogs that were edible were kept in the smokehouse. He also raised chickens. The family never had to worry about food. They had to pluck and clean the chickens for Grandma to cook. Mom said when it rained, she would get wet because there were holes in the roof. They were accustomed to putting pots down to catch the water so that the rain would not get on the bed.

When you think of a grandmother, you typically think of being spoiled by her, however, I did not have this relationship with my grandmother. One thing that I can say about my grandmother is that she was an awesome seamstress. She could make anything from clothes to drapes and curtains. One day I had to make this jumper for my home economics class. She helped me so much that I got and A on this project.

When growing up as a young teenager, the only way that my mother could go out was if she was with one of her older sisters. After my father met my mother, he pretended to be dating one of my mother's older sisters, but he was actually going out with my mother. When they went on a date, as soon as they got out of sight, they would trade seats in Daddy's truck. They would drop my aunt off at her boyfriend's house and continue on their date. When it was time for them to go home, they would pick my aunt up from her boyfriend's house and my aunt would sit in the middle again, just like when they had left.

One day my father came to my grandparent's house. Grandma said, "Are you here to pick up Jessica?" My father replied, "No, I am here to pick up Renee." My grandmother said, "Renee is not dating anyone." Then my father said to her, "Renee is pregnant with my child." My mom said you would have thought the world was coming to an end that day. This was not a good day in my Grandparents house. They were disappointed because my mom was not telling the truth. In those days, the only thing to happen was for my parents to get married. That is exactly what happened. My Grandparents were so upset because my mother did not tell them the truth. My mother was only seventeen years old, and my father was thirty-four. Grandma was so outraged that she refused to sign for mother off to get married. My grandfather was the one who ended up signing her off to get married.

After they were married, my mother stayed with my grandparents for about three weeks. Something happened on that third week and my mom was forced to go live with her husband. I can only imagine how afraid my mother felt. This was her first time being away her brothers, sisters and parents. My father, having been married before, already had a house. When he got home one day, my mother was at his house. I asked my mother why she didn't go to my father's house when they first got married. She told me that she didn't want to leave home yet. This time she had no choice but to go live with her husband.

I think that they did it just because she was

pregnant. Do not get me wrong: my mother was wrong too for going out with my father, because he was much older than she was. I wonder if her parents ever took into consideration that it was only a matter of time before he started to abuse their daughter. I believe my grandmother was concerned, but not as much as my Grandfather.

My father had done everything he wanted to do while he was young. My mother had lived a sheltered life. My father had achieved his mission. He had a young, naïve child that he could manipulate and mold into the woman that he always wanted. I guess my father thought that she could give him as many children as he desired.

Every year after the first baby, my mother was pregnant. She had three children in three years. The doctor told her after the third child that she could not have any more. She had had cesarean sections with all of her children. Another pregnancy would mean risking her life. Again, because my mother was so willing to please her husband, she got pregnant. They said I was a miracle baby. The only reason my mom did not get pregnant again was because she had fibroid tumors that led to an emergency hysterectomy. My youngest brother and I are only eleven months apart.

My mother said that my father took good care of

her and always took care of us. My father was a farmer. Being a farmer, he was not making enough money to take care of the family, so he went to work at Gwaltney's meat packing plant as a ham boner.

Everything was going well for the first seven years of their marriage, and then things changed. My mom was a stay-at-home mother until I was in the first grade, and then she went to work at Gwaltney's with my father as a ham boner also. During those first seven years of marriage, my mother became an adult. While at work, she met friends and started doing things with them. We noticed that my mother and father were not nice to one and another. I think this changed because my mother had new friends at work and he did not have that control over her anymore so it seemed liked the tension between them was very high. Sometimes they were not nice to each other but they never abused us. We were disciplined when we were disobedient. Statistics say if your parents came from an abusive home, they will likely abuse their children, but this is not true in all cases. My parents instilled morals and values, encouraged high self-esteem, and made us strive to always do our best at everything that we did. They taught us to respect everyone, especially older people. Although my father was illiterate and my mother had to drop out in the tenth grade, education for us was top priority. They wanted better for us. They felt that education was the key to success.

I spoke with my mother about her childhood. At first, everything was fine, and then she just started to cry. She said to me, "Baby, I just can't talk about the abuse anymore. The scars are so deep."

Like I said before, there is a favorite child in every family, especially in larger families. Some parents do show favoritism and, unfortunately, that's what they want the siblings to see. In other situations, they don't intend to show favoritism, it unconsciously happens. I know my parents did not consciously show favoritism. I was the youngest, so my siblings may have thought my parents showed favoritism. Both of my parents in probably would not have believed my mother's horrible account of the things she had done to her as a child.

The elementary school that we attended was behind my grandparent's house. We would go to her house until my parents got off work. I can remember one incident when my grandmother thought we had stolen money from her. When I was in elementary school, grades were from kindergarden to the seventh grade. One day she came and got all of us out of school because she thought we had taken some money from her. I was really scared.

The neighbor across the street saw and heard her

screaming at us, so she called our mother at work. We were so happy to see Mama because we knew everything was going to be all right at that moment.

My mother and father paid a live-in babysitter to take care of us from that day on. Nita Holloman took such good care of us. I was so sad because we had gotten older and my older sister began taking care of us.

CHAPTER 2

$\mathscr{D}$ealing with $\mathscr{O}$besity

L ooking back over my life, I know that even when I was two, God had a special calling on my life. Matthew 17:20 states, "And then Jesus answered and said: faithless and perverse generation, how long shall I am with you? How long shall I suffer you? Bring him hither to me." My parents would have given their own lives for me. Just as in days of old, God was still God, so I woke up.

Throughout my childhood, I had problems with obesity. However, my mother was very supportive. She made sure that I was well dressed for school. I can remember hearing the other children in the neighborhood playing outside. It sounded as though they were having a wonderful time. I watched from the window. My parents questioned me about not going outside. I often used studying as an excuse. I don't know how I got away with it, because it was summertime. Being obese can affect you physically, psychologically, and emotionally. If you don't have a strong support system, it can cause a person to look for love in the wrong places. You just want to be accepted for you.

As a teenager, older people often commented on my appearance. They would tell me how pretty I was, but how I was just so big. Can you imagine someone giving you a compliment and an insult in the same breath? My mother kept my self-esteem up. She would say, "Don't worry about what those people are saying. Remember you have a pretty face, and I would die to have those pretty legs." She complimented me on being so smart in school and told me that most of the children were jealous of me. She always told me to keep my head up. She made it known that, as I got older, it was going to get harder, but to just remember that I came from a strong bloodline. Even though she told me all those things, I was dying inside. It was my own personal ordeal. I didn't know how to deal with all the mixed emotions.

Elementary school was from kindergarten to the seventh grade. I had the biggest breasts in the entire school, teachers included. Can you imagine having larger breasts than your elementary school teachers?

My plight was later overshadowed by teen pregnancies in school. I wasn't happy that these girls were pregnant, but it did take the negative attention off me. The other students came to know me not only as the fat girl, but also the smart girl. Some of the students would hang around me just to cheat on tests. I didn't approve of the cheating, but I had gained an appearance of popularity.

Some say that obesity is a disease. I believe that it is hereditary. I think people overeat when they are stressed. Growing up, I certainly had my share of that. People eat just to fill a void. I don't know about a void, but I ate because it made me feel good. It was comforting.

As far as heredity, genes affect a huge part of a person's body build. They also affect a huge number of weight-related chemical processes in the body. Metabolic metabolism, fat storage, and hormones, just to name a few, are all influenced by our genetic makeup. Studies of adopted children have proven that those who are adopted tend to develop the same weight problems as their biological parents. Infants born to overweight moms have been found to be less active and to gain more weight by the age of three. This indicates a possible inborn drive to conserve energy.

We lived on a farm and ate everything. We grew our own fruits and vegetables, such as green beans, butter beans, salad, kale, watermelon, and cantaloupe. Most everything we ate was fried. We ate my dad's homemade sausage from pigs for breakfast every morning, along with eggs and toast. Can you imagine the amount of fat consumed in one week with this type of breakfast?

I didn't know until I was in college about the different types of fats (good fats and bad fats). For instance, saturated fats are the worst kind of fat. People who are overweight or obese should limit their total fat intake to no more than 30 percent of total calories.

Let's get started on the different types of fats. Polyunsaturated and monounsaturated fats may help lower your blood cholesterol level when you eat them in place of saturated fats. When I was growing up, this was unheard of. I didn't know which ones were good for me and which ones were bad. One day during my yearly physical, I was told that I had to stop eating fried food, sweets, soft drinks, and a few more things. I was totally shocked. I grew up with the motto, "Clean your plate." I was a good girl, so I cleaned my plate every time. Now here I was being told that my nutritional habits were not only wrong, but they were putting my health in danger.

From that day on, it was instilled in my head to do better with my child. I don't want my daughter growing up the way I did. People say, "What you don't know won't hurt you." But that's not true. The lack of knowledge will kill you! Saturated fats are the main dietary cause of high blood pressure and high cholesterol. There are several different types of cholesterol—good and bad cholesterol. We need to know which ones are good and which ones are bad. According to Diabetes.org, we all need some cholesterol (a waxy fat-like substance that is found in foods and produced by the body) in our blood to keep our organs working. There are different types of cholesterol. Some help to keep the arteries clear and some can cause buildup that leads to heart disease. For people with diabetes, the extra glucose in their blood sticks to cholesterol particles and clogs the arteries, causing high blood pressure, strokes, and heart attacks. The FDA has made some important changes on how they label food items. There are at least five foods that can lower your cholesterol, and they are almonds, oatmeal, fish, red wine, and soy. African Americans need to have yearly checkups that include a cholesterol check. Do not be afraid to ask your doctor questions if you do not understand.

The American Heart Association recommends that you limit your saturated fat intake to 71 percent of total calories each day. The FDA passed a regulation requiring trans fat to be listed on the nutrition label by January 2, 2006. Changing the labels was a positive step, but most people still do not understand what the differences are between good fats and bad fats. They have to be taught. Maybe the government should send some type of information explaining the differences. African Americans need to be educated more than any other ethnic group. Most of us were taught by our parents that the food that we ate all our lives was good for us. By the age of twenty, my health and quality of life had gone downhill. My first physical, at the local health department, reported that my cholesterol was very high. I was told to change my eating habits or risk having to take medications.

I decided to conduct a random survey to see if people knew their cholesterol levels. This survey asked approximately one hundred people if they knew what levels were normal, borderline, or high. The findings were shocking. Of the one hundred people surveyed, 98 percent of them did not have a clue and 2 percent of them had just had a physical. I was astonished that all the African Americans surveyed had no idea what the levels were. We have to educate people about cholesterol and high blood pressure because they are the two main killers in the African American community. I like to call them silent killers, because you don't really know they're there until it's much too late. Other ethnic groups demonstrated the same lack of knowledge. The participants were given nutritional information. Hopefully, a seed was planted to get them to think more about healthy living.

I observed each participant place the information in his or her wallet or purse. It was a joy to see that people wanted the information. I had not only educated them but also inspired and empowered some to change their lives. Originally, I didn't think to include cholesterol in this book, but in my spirit, I felt that people needed to know.

I had some mixed feelings about the survey with reference to the willingness of the participants. The responses were somewhat frustrating. African Americans who are at risk the most were the least interested of all persons surveyed! I would think that they would have wanted to know the most. Older participants were equally uninterested. It is sad to say, but other ethnic groups were more concerned.

I could not understand why some people did not want information that could potentially save their life. The reason I am writing this book is because I want people to be educated about different things about their health. I don't want anyone to go through what I continue to endure to this day. As a society, we need to share as much information to help one another as possible. Today, I was meditating about some of the negative attitudes that we received while doing the cholesterol survey. God put in my spirit, "Lean not on your own understanding, trust him in all thy ways and he will direct thy path" (Proverbs 3:5–6). At that moment, I was not as concerned about the negative responses that we received because God already knew how the survey was going to turn out. When I read that Scripture, it made me realize that God had it all in control. He knew who was going to participate and who was not. I just moved on to the next person. Never in my wildest dreams did I think that I would be writing a book about the past ten years of my life. Philippians 4:13 says, "I can do all things through Christ who strengthens me." All we have to do is believe in Jesus Christ, even when times get tough. Those are the things that make us the strongest.

When God has something for us to do, the Devil always has his little demons to try to stop our blessings, but we must try not to get into the flesh. The flesh and the spirit are constantly fighting each other. For example, my daughter's best friend was saved in my house; ever since, the Devil has been messing with her, but I plead the blood of Jesus over her. My daughter is sixteen and I told her she is responsible for her now. The young people today really have a hard time because they are looking at the things of the world and entertainers on the television and want to be like them. The Word of God says we live in the world but we are not part of the world. It is hard to try to explain this to my daughter because her mind isn't that mature just yet, but I know with my husband and my prayers, she is going to be just fine.

When God gives you an assignment, it does not matter how you feel. That task has to be fulfilled. I made a promise to God that I would work on my book every day. I have succeeded in doing that because I fear God more than I fear anyone else. One night, I had fallen asleep and I looked at the clock, and it looked like it said twenty after twelve. I was just about in tears, but when I looked again, it was eleven twenty. You should have seen me get my computer to be sure that I did something with my book before the day ended.

July 13, 2006, was a very rough day for me because my father had died two years ago on this date. I still cannot believe he is gone. God evidently wanted him more than we did. On July 31, I received some of my surveys back from a friend. They had all been done wrong. I did not get upset because it didn't matter. He is my brother in Christ, so I fussed him out in the name of Jesus. He came over to get some more surveys to make them right. That's what happens when you are a true man of God. He fixed his mistake and he did not get mad, which is what you are supposed to do. I admire him so much. God had just put Greg in our lives. He is my brother in Christ, and I also call him my biological brother. I can call him any time of night, and he is there for me. I thank God for him.

When God does something, he does not make any mistakes. That is how good of a God we serve. Recently, I went to my neurologist who ordered a lipid panel, which is a cholesterol test. I could not believe it when the results came back. My cholesterol was good. I do not eat fried foods, sweets, soft drinks, or peanuts. I read all the labels on all my foods. I do not eat fast foods. My husband and daughter say I am so meticulous. I have to be, if I want to stay healthy. Cholesterol is hereditary. My mother is on a cholesterol pill and when my father was living, he had a problem with his cholesterol. When I went back to my neurologist, I knew that he was going to put me on a cholesterol pill cholesterol but he did not because my cholesterol was good. I thought due to me having two mini strokes, and the history of my mother and father having high cholesterol mines was going to be high, but it wasn't I was so happy.

Even if my doctor put me on a cholesterol pill, it was okay because I know how far I have come from taking about twenty to thirty pills a day. You have to keep reading to believe me.

CHAPTER 3

Father Being Diagnosed with Cancer

My father often complained about being in pain and took medication. He was constantly going to the doctor. They could never find anything wrong with him. One day, he complained more than usual. My mother got worried and took him to another doctor. When my father spoke with the doctor about his symptoms, he was immediately admitted into the hospital. After a week of testing, my mother received a call from the doctor one night at about 9:30 p.m. The news about the test was not good. I remember hearing my mother screaming, "No, I can't believe he has cancer!" She was in complete shock and so were we.

It was the spring of my last year in high school. I

was preparing for college. My family was so excited because I was going to be the first college student. My father had been diagnosed with lymphoma. We didn't know anything about lymphoma. We were so afraid that Dad would die at any time. The doctor explained that this was a slow-progressing cancer. We were told that my dad would have to take chemotherapy to stop the growth of the cancer cells. My mother, being limited in education, did not understand much about the disease.

Lymphoma is a cancer of the lymphatic system. The lymphatic system carries fluid and white blood cells throughout body. The purpose of the lymphatic system is to fight infections. The day that I was told about the cancer, I walked to the store down the highway and bought so much candy. However, I didn't even eat any of it. Looking back now, I realize that this was the start of me dealing with my obesity spiraling out of control. I think this was my way of trying to deal with the devastating news about my dad.

Suddenly my mother was faced with decisions, so many decisions. She wondered how she would be able to provide for us and her two grandchildren. I really don't know what I would have done had I been in her shoes. My oldest brother was in the navy. He could not get home right away. I took the role of speaking to the doctors because my mom had limited understanding of all the medical jargon. I was eighteen years old, and I handled all the business affairs for my parents. They knew to pay the most important bills, which were the electric bill and the mortgage. Our house went into foreclosure several times until a white friend of my parents literally purchased our house and held the deed. At that time, we had a wood heater and other neighbors in our community would make sure we had enough wood.

Before my father was diagnosed with cancer, he had been a heavy smoker. Actually, both of my parents were heavy smokers. When we found out that Daddy had lymphoma, I thought he had lung cancer because he smoked so much. Two years earlier, my father's brother had been diagnosed with cancer and died. He too had been a heavy smoker. As soon as my father found out that he had cancer, he immediately stopped smoking. The doctor did not have to tell him to stop. He stopped cold turkey.

My family could not afford the chemotherapy treatments, so Dad had to go the clinic at Norfolk General Hospital. My mother was faced with another dilemma: how was she going to get him to and from treatment because she had to continue to work to support the family? It was one month before my high school graduation. I decided I was not going to college. I planned to stay home and get a full-time job to help take care of my niece and nephew. My parents would not hear of it. They were adamant that nothing was going to ruin the dream of me getting a college education. By the time that he needed to start the chemotherapy, summer had come. I could take my father to his appointments and work to help my mother with the bills. I think when a family is faced with an unexpected tragedy like a father being diagnosed with cancer, everyone should come together for the good of the family. That's exactly what happened in our case. All of this was stressful, and I dealt with it the way I usually did.

My dad's doctor started him on an aggressive regiment of chemotherapy to give him the best possible chance of survival and beating the disease. Dad had to go for treatments three times a week: Mondays, Wednesdays, and Fridays. I would ensure that Dad's paperwork was filled out correctly. I also made sure that they treated him with respect, just as if he had private insurance. Even though my mother was the only one working, she still had to pay something for him to go to the clinic. It was not free, and if it was free, he still should have been treated just like the next person who had private insurance. The process of me taking my father to his appointments became routine. Each time I took my dad to the doctor, it was always something new about his fate. I felt totally helpless because nothing I said would lift his spirits. I had to make sure he would always be encouraged, that everything was going to be all right. I felt helpless, frustrated, and sad. There was a rage inside of me. I wondered why this had to happen to my dad. I just began to withdraw into my own world but was trying not to let my father see me sad.

Being in college full time and having the responsibility of my dad's care began to take a toll on me. My grades were suffering. Sometimes, I would be on the highway at three or four o'clock in the morning and have an eight o'clock class. The advantage of going to a small university, Virginia Union University in my case, is that your professors know you personally. They recognized the change in my performance as well as my excessive absences. I can remember one professor in particular, my psychology professor, pulling me aside one day. He asked me about the sudden low test scores, lack of homework assignments, and excessive absences. Strange, but no one was asking about the constant weight gain.

CHAPTER 4

Leon, the Love of My Life

*I*t was the summer of 1985, and I was working as the assistant manager at a 7-Eleven Convenience Store. There was a family that lived across the street. My roommate at the time said, "Girl have you seen those two good-looking guys that live over there across the street?"

I said, "Yeah, I've seen them. That little small one just drinks and smokes marijuana."

She said, "But they're fine!"

I said, "Yeah, they're fine, but I don't want to have anything to do with either of them."

I have always felt that we never know what God has in store for us, so we have to learn to not judge people. If I had judged him, I would have never married the love of my life, my husband Leon.

Leon is truly a man beyond men. God definitely knew what he was doing when he put us together. I had been leery about talking to anyone about my life experiences because my heart had been broken by someone who I thought was the love of my life. He was in the military and was just using me for everything he could get from me. I would send him sneakers and tapes and would fly to see him. Once I flew all the way to Colorado just to be with him.

When I finally let him go, or shall I say when he let me go, I realized that it wasn't love at all. We have to be careful in this world when it comes to love because that *love* word can lead to big trouble. Love is an action word, something you put into action. You don't just say it; you show it. You show it by what you do for others and what they do for you. Love is the effort behind your kind actions toward others. The Word of God says you are supposed to love each other. The Word of God also says to love your neighbors and brethren as you love yourself. That means we are to love people the way that God loves us, which means it should be an unconditional love. Unfortunately, my first love was very, very selfish.

My last year of college, I was flying all over the place while trying to be with him. I made many bad decisions. He really didn't care anything about me. I was infatuated by his military clothes, since I had a thing for men wearing military uniforms. I admit that was a weakness. I love to see them in their military dress and fatigues. There was nothing like seeing a handsome man looking sharp in a military uniform. I was truly in love, but he didn't love me. I paid a high price for being in love. It really made it hard for me to deal with daily life.

He had planned to stay with me before going overseas for three years in Germany. He had been given thirty days of leave before he had to depart. He planned to spend fifteen days with me. The other fifteen days were to be spent with his family in Chattanooga, Tennessee. However, he did not. I sat home and waited for a phone call. I didn't even go to class. I never got the call. I called his mother's house in Chattanooga. She would always say that he was out. He never returned my calls. I later found out from one of his friends that he was still dating his girlfriend in Chattanooga. This girl was in the military and was stationed in Colorado Springs with him. He was also dating a third girl. He was dating the three of us at the same time. He was playing us. He didn't drink and he didn't smoke, and those were the qualities that attracted me to him. He had all the qualities that I was looking for. He came from a good family and appeared to have good morals.

However, that wasn't what God had for me. We have to be careful about what we want and what God wants for us. He lacked one big quality, and that was he didn't have the ability to love a single woman.

Ultimately, he ended up breaking my heart. I dropped out of college because of him. I didn't tell my parents until about six months later. My mom and dad were absolutely heartbroken. Finishing college was something that they wanted me to do. Not only did my boyfriend let me down, but more importantly, I let my parents down. Most of all, I let myself down. I handled it in my usual way I would not eat which caused me to gain weight. Words could not express the emotions that I felt. My dad had said that he wanted to see me, his baby girl, graduate from college before he left this world.

I met my husband when I was working as the assistant manager at 7-Eleven, right across the street from where he and his family lived. He would come in first thing when I opened the store at six o'clock in the morning. He would come in with his eyes bloodshot red. He would try to buy beer, and I would never sell it to him out of fear that he would get behind the wheel of a car and take his own life, or the life of others, from being so intoxicated. Every time, no matter what I would say, he was always polite. His famous words to me were, "Okay, Miss Lady," and he would leave the store.

My roommate approached me one day because I guess she had noticed that one of the brothers had a crush on me. He at the time was not attractive to me because he had qualities that I didn't want in a man. He drank and he smoked cigarettes and marijuana. But it turned out that meeting him was the best thing to ever happen to me.

Until you really sit down and get to know someone, you don't know what situations have caused him or her to do the things that he or she does. The main reason most people drink, use drugs, have promiscuous sex, and do other self-destructive things is because they are trying to cover up much deeper problems that are going on with them. This was the case with my husband. He had issues with his family. Every family has issues, but there were some really deep issues that were going on within his family. There was no security or stability.

One day, the girl that worked with me said, "Girl, that guy likes you." I asked which one she was talking about, and she told me the smallest one. This so happened to be the same guy who would come in every morning trying to buy more alcohol. I learned that he was the head cook at a restaurant called The Family Fish House. One night after work, my girlfriend and I decided to go to The Family Fish House. We made a bet to see if he really liked her or me. We got all dressed up and I was decked out. Both of us looked good that night.

The waitress came over and took our order. She was a student at Virginia Commonwealth University and happened to be a close friend of Leon's. I asked her if she would tell Leon to come over to our table for a minute. He came over and I greeted him then asked how he was doing. He said, "Hi." I told him that I loved fried oysters, so he cooked me some fried oysters and some french fries with coleslaw. I didn't drink so I had a nonalcoholic daiquiri. At the end of the dinner, I told the waitress to give Leon my number and to tell him to call me. I also told her to tell him that I had my own place. I knew he got off at about one o'clock in the morning, but I told her to tell him that he could call me at any time. Some men like to try to play hard to get, so he didn't call me that night. He called me the next day.

Leon and I talked on the phone for a while, and then I asked him if he wanted to come over to my place. He came over, and I got to know him on a more personal level. When I say, "I got to know him on a more personal level," I mean by conversation—not sexually. I said to myself, "This man is a good man. All he needs is someone to expose him to a different life."

He had never been out the city of Richmond. He had never been to the Tidewater region, DC, Maryland, or any other places. I exposed him to all of that, and opened up a whole different world to him.

Initially, Leon felt a little intimidated by me because he only had some high school education. He had dropped out in the eleventh grade. Most of my friends were college graduates or had some college education. He felt like he didn't equal up. He didn't like being around when my friends came to visit, especially one girl who was a very close friend from high school. She lived here in Richmond at the time and was a police officer. She went to the police academy right out of high school, but she didn't have any college education. My roommate was in college, and at first, Leon had a problem with it. We would have friends over and I would notice that Leon would be very uncomfortable. I had a talk with him about it one day. He said to me that these were not the type of people he was used to hanging around. The type of people Leon use to hang with were thugs or people from the streets. He always hung around the projects with people who were use to not doing anything. Leon wasn't doing anything with life except for working. One thing I can say about my husband he was always a hard worker and took care of all his responsibilities. As a result of his willing and unselfish heart, Leon had several cars repossessed that he could have easily afforded, if family situation had been different.

After we dated for about a year or so, Leon told me that he really loved me. I told him that I loved him too. I told him that he could either continue on this path of being unhappy or he could come live with me and that I would help him out of his situation. I knew that my parents were going to have a fit since I would be living with a man and was not married, but I concluded that I was grown and I wanted to help Leon.

One night I left him the keys to my apartment. I told him that if he moved in, I was going to help him keep his car. I also told him that he would have to make some decisions and change his living situation. That's exactly what he did. He still had his same friends, but they respected me. They would not come to my house smoking weed or drinking. They tried to, but I quickly got them straight and I got him straight really quickly too.

Leon slowly began to stop hanging with fake friends and they started saying, "Man, you don't do anything anymore." They weren't going anywhere in life, so of course they didn't want to see him going anywhere either. They saw that he had someone that really cared for him, someone that really loved him for him.

Leon also accepted me for me. He accepted me for the size that I was. He also accepted my educational background and the fact that I would not tolerate the drugs. One thing I can say about people is that they are not going to change anything until they are ready to make changes. It doesn't matter how much you fuss or how much you talk to that person. If that person isn't willing to make those changes in his life, it does not matter what you say to him. Leon on the other hand, decided to make those changes in his life.

I finally told my parents six months after he had moved in that I had a boyfriend. My parents were very, very strict, especially my father. In his eyes, nobody was good enough for his baby girl. I told Leon that he needed to meet my parents. I told him upfront that my dad in particular was going to ask him a lot of questions like if he went to school, what church he went to, where he worked, where his mother worked, where his father worked, etc.

My dad really surprised me when he met Leon. He saw something in Leon that he liked. He liked the fact that this was a man that loved his daughter, this was a man that had respect, and this was a man who did not mind working. These are all the qualities that my husband possesses. It is awesome to have someone like that, especially with what we had to be faced with later on in our relationship. God already knew what was going to happen.

The old saying is true that opposites attract. That is exactly what happened to me and my wonderful husband. He's the total opposite of me and I'm the total opposite of him. He is laid back, quiet, and reserved and not really a people person. However, once he gets to know you, he'll talk a little more. His strengths are my weaknesses, and my strengths are his weaknesses. Together we are strong. Though our backgrounds are different, Leon and I complement each other very well. Leon came from a single-parent home. He was raised by his mother because his father was not around. The only father figure Leon had that he could look up to was his uncle. Leon loved his mother very much and would do anything for her. At first, I had a little trouble accepting this fact because I felt as that he loved his mother more than he loved me. Then I really thought about it. If this man loves his mother so much and does so many nice things for her, then I'm sure he will do the same for my mother. I was right. Leon's relationship with his mother has taught me so much. I realized that this quality of a man loving his mother and respecting her no matter what was very commendable. He was going to pass those same qualities on to his offspring. I also learned that you have to love your mother regardless of whether you get along with her or not. I can say that watching how my husband loves, honors, and respects his mother, no matter what differences they may have, taught me a valuable lesson. This is one of the many things that I appreciate him teaching me, without him even knowing. This is also one of the many reasons that I am so grateful and deeply in love with my husband.

CHAPTER 5

My Greatest Accomplishment, Tiffany

The greatest accomplishment in my life first was having a child. Honestly, I didn't want a child. However, I knew that having unprotected sex with my husband put me at risk for pregnancy. I took that on, and it was an accomplishment for me.

It was not easy carrying Tiffany. It appeared that my health started to decline with the pregnancy. I had to have an emergency C-section. Six months later, I had to have a partial hysterectomy, because a fibroid tumor grew, covering my entire uterus. I was in excruciating pain. Just the thought of a hysterectomy, having my female reproductive organs removed, can be a very mental thing, especially with the realization of an early menopause. I was so young. I was twenty-six when I had the hysterectomy, and that was my fifth major surgery. One of my ovaries was left in so that it could produce the needed estrogen. Six months after having the partial, I was back for a complete hysterectomy. This means that my cervix, my uterus, and my ovaries were all removed.

I was twenty-six with a brand-new baby, with no female reproductive organs, going through postpartum depression and an estrogen imbalance. Because of the hormone imbalance, I was put on an artificial estrogen patch, which caused me to gain a lot of weight. I gained nineteen pounds while I was carrying Tiffany. I was two hundred eighty-nine pounds when we got married. I had gone up to 309 pounds. After I had her, I lost some weight. I was down to 270 pounds, but I didn't stay that size for long.

Tiffany is a major accomplishment for me. I thank God that she's a young lady and will be soon be eighteen. She has proven to be such a wonderful child. Now she is proving to be such a wonderful woman.

It was hard for me to get past the bitterness that I had toward her paternal grandparents, uncles, and aunts. I got to a point where I realized I had to let it go. They are the ones who were missing out on such an adorable child's life. They were the ones who are going to suffer in the long run. I still have to be a parent; I still have to tell her what is right and what is wrong when it comes to her grandparents, uncles, and aunts. It wasn't easy, but one thing I can say is that I never talked bad about them to her. Even when she was angry and bitter toward them, I would always remind her that they were still her family. I told her to be thankful that her father and I worked very hard so that she could have, and she should be thankful for what she has.

Being a parent is the most awesome experience a human being can have in a lifetime. Children don't ask to come in this world. If you have problems like I did, you must always be a parent first. She realized as a teenager that I am a parent first. She knew that I could be her friend, her best friend, but I am always her parent first. Children need structure, discipline, and rules. They might pout, fuss, and complain, but they need rules. They need someone to say, "No you can't do that. These are the consequences of your behavior; this is what's going to happen to you." Children want and need that in their lives. We as parents have to understand that.

Parents need to act like parents. We need to treat our children with respect and listen to them. There is so much going on in the world today and we don't want them to be ignorant about issues, such as sex or what is going on in the world. We have to be open and honest with them. One thing that I can say about children is that they are very honest. They sometimes go through a lying phase, but when you really ask them for the bare-naked truth, most children will keep it real. That's what I love so much about children, the fact that they keep it real.

Tiffany happens to be one those children who keep it real when she voices her opinion. We allowed her to voice her opinion and always listened to what she had to say. As parents, we need to listen to what our children are saying. We need to get all into their business. It is important to know their friends and who they are hanging out with. I feel that parents are falling short in that area. There is no manual on how to raise children. Tiffany was raised with the some of the same morals and values as my parents instilled in me and Leon's mother and grandparents instilled in him.

Every child is different and needs to be treated according to his or her own individual differences. Tiffany is our only child, but if we had others, we would still love each one of them. Parents with multiple children may say they love them all the same, but really you cannot love them all the exact same because they are all different. Thus, you treat them in different ways. Tiffany has many of my traits as well as her father's.

For instance, she was never into Barbie dolls. I often wondered why she never got excited about getting a Barbie for Christmas or birthdays. She always wanted a tool set like her daddy. She was never into that girly stuff. She was always into hands-on activities and learning new things. We always gave her books for Christmas also. I read to her while I was pregnant and when she was very small. I would rub my stomach and I would say, "Tiffany, I am reading you this book." Tiffany has become a strong writer. She loves to write just like her mother. Her daddy likes hands-on type of activities. Tiffany is good at hands-on activities and loves putting stuff together. Personally, I'd rather pay someone to put things together for me if I was married to my awesone husband. My husband has saved us a lot of money, because we did not have to hire anyone to fix the problem.

Tiffany has inherited the best of both of us. She doesn't hang around negative people and she has made very good decisions in her life, even while living through all the complications of my life for the past eleven years. She could have made some very bad decisions. She could have easily gotten caught up with the depressions of my life and spiraled downward. She could have ended up on drugs, been promiscuous, and done an array of negative things, but she didn't. I am very thankful for that. I feel that she is definitely my number one accomplishment. I love her so much. I love her with everything in me, and I am thankful that God gave her to me. She's such a special child.

We need to tell our children that we love them because they go through that phase of thinking that we are always fussing with them to get them to clean their room or do their chores and you get that, "You don't love me! All you do is fuss at me!" They need to know that we love them. They need to know that you will be the first to step up to the plate to help them in any situation.

There are two things you don't mess with, depending on who you ask. You don't mess with their money and you don't mess with their offspring. If you really want to see the bad side of a mother, mess with her child. I remember when Tiffany was about four and in private school, and we had to pay extra for the computer classes. We paid extra every week for her to be in this class. The director's child and Tiffany did not get along. They were like oil and water; they did not mix. The little girl bit Tiffany a couple of times. It's hard to explain to a four-year-old not to bite back. I had a meeting with the mother, the director. I told her that we do not advocate fighting or that type of behavior. Though Tiffany did do some things to provoke the girl, she didn't bite her. Biting is a behavior that is learned. The director said she tried to discipline the girl by putting her in timeout and taking away her playtime. The biting did not stop. I had another meeting with the other parent. I told her, "If your child bites Tiffany again, I'm going to tell her to bite her back." Being a parent is very difficult and some of the decisions we make are not good ones. Under no circumstance should I have told my daughter to be a part of negative behavior. As a result, the little girl bit Tiffany again, but this time Tiffany bit her back. The little girl never bit Tiffany again after that.

Tiffany turned out to be a beautiful young woman. One thing I asked God to do for me when I was sick was to let me live long enough for her to be able to take care of her herself. He did that and much more.

CHAPTER 6

The Gastric Bypass

*A*fter going through depression, dropping *out* behind what I thought was love, falling in true love, getting married, and having a child, I finally went back to Virginia Union University to finish my college education—just as I had promised myself, and my parents more importantly. Once I graduated from college, I had many job opportunities. My first job was working at a bank in a call center. I applied for this job before obtaining my degree, but I never received a call back. I applied again and was called back after I had my degree. I only stayed about a year at my second job. The next job was a benefit analyst at a company called Trigon, Blue Cross Blue Shield one of the world's largest insurance companies. During this time,

I was having problems due to being overweight. The most serious of my problems were sleep apnea, high blood pressure, high cholesterol, and a knee replacement.

I'll never forget June 1996. It seems like it was just yesterday. I went to my primary-care physician; I was experiencing very bad migraine headaches. I had chronic bronchitis. My doctor was very blunt with me. He said, "Lynette, I know you don't want to have any more surgeries because you have already had several, but if you don't get the weight off significantly and keep it off, I cannot promise you how much longer you're going to live." I sat in his office and cried and cried hysterically. Finally, I told him that I could not make that decision. I needed to pray, talk to my husband, and talk to my family before giving an answer.

Initially, both my husband and my family were totally against the surgery. My doctor suggested surgery because I had already been on several diets. I would lose weight and then gain back more. I was now faced with a life-or-death decision. I had an enlarged heart, because it was trying to keep up with a body that was much larger than it should have been. Being a Christian, I went to God and said, "I know, God, that you can do all things, and I know that I can't make this decision without you, and you have to show me with the natural eye (that means that I have to see it myself on paper) that it's okay for me to have this surgery."

That's exactly what God did. Approximately three to four weeks after talking with God, I had insurance claims coming across my desk several times a week. It included all the information I needed to know, so I decided to have the surgery. God had prepared me. What I did not know was that God would allow me to suffer the next eleven years of my life.

It was January 6, 1997, when I had the gastric bypass surgery. Later that same year, I realized that I was not going to be able to go back to work. I tried to go back for about a month, but due to all the complications, I soon realized that I would be unable to return. This was a very harsh reality.

By October 1997, I had lost two hundred pounds. No one should ever lose two hundred pounds in ten months. This was mainly due to not being able to eat much following the surgery.

It took from January 6, 1997, until April of 1999 for me to get approved for disability through social security. So many people are denied social security, which is money that they put into the system. That's the purpose of paying into the system. My attorney called and asked if I wanted my medical records. I initially said no, but later told her to go ahead and send them to me. My medical records weighed thirty pounds. I didn't have to go to court. The judge made a decision based on my records alone. I never planned to rely on social security until after I retired. I never even imagined that I would end up needing it at such an early age.

So many things have happened to me as a result of the surgery. It's no wonder that my medical records weighed thirty pounds. The main reasons I was approved to have the surgery were acidosis (acid reflux), sleep apnea, narcolepsy, degenerative disc disease, and a cystic gall bladder. The gastric bypass is a surgery where your whole digestive tract is reconstructed, from your esophagus to your large intestine. Three-fourths of the stomach is stapled off into a pouch so that you are not able to eat large portions of food at one time. When you first have the surgery your stomach is the size of a medicine cup that is given to a patient when one is in the hospital. This surgery is not without possible complications. One of those complications is malabsorption, which leads to vitamin deficiency, dehydration, chronic diarrhea, chronic constipation, and chronic pain. They really didn't go into details about this actually happening. These were just a few of the complications discussed with me. A small percentage of patients might experience some complications.

Keep in mind that when a physician talks to you, he or she usually discusses complications that fall within the normal cases, not the extreme cases. I was told that if I were to have any of these complications, that they would eventually go away. Well, my complications never went away. I was an extreme case. Unfortunately, I found myself in that small percentage of people who experiences complications due to the gastric bypass.

Following surgery, I was put on a ventilator for three days because I could not breathe on my own. I had to be on a liquid diet for the next three weeks. My diet was slowly increased to shredded meats, such as ham and turkey. I really could not tolerate any main course foods for the next three years. I could not eat bread, steak, or any other main-course foods. I had to chew my food completely, almost to a liquid form. This meant I had to chew each bite about thirty to forty times in order to break it down to be digestible before swallowing. The area where they connected the stomach and the esophagus was so tight. Almost nothing would go down. I had about sixty to seventy staples and numerous stitches after the surgery. I could not keep anything down. Can you imagine throwing up with all those staple and stitches? The X-rays showed that the connection to the stomach was in fact too tight. I had to go through a procedure called an endoscopy. An endoscopy is a test where they take a tube and go down your throat through your esophagus to your stomach. This test is performed by a gastro-intestinal specialist, a doctor who specializes in everything that deals with the stomach.

I had nine endoscopies within a three-month period. Endoscopies are usually only administered every three to five years. I spent a large portion of the first year after the surgery in the hospital. Finally, they injected the opening with steroids. In April 1997, it remained open and allowed fluid to pass through. However, I had been so long without being able to eat that when I did eat, even very small amounts of food could not be tolerated. I had to take vitamins because my body could no longer absorb nutrients as it had before the bypass. In my case, I was not able to absorb any food. I could not keep down any food and was going to the bathroom with severe diarrhea five to ten times a day. I was totally depleted of all my electrolytes.

Thus, I spent a large portion of the first year after the surgery in the hospital. Ultimately, a revision of the bypass had to be done. They had to add back part of my large intestine with the hope that I would then be able to absorb nutrients. However, this did not work. After this surgery, they put drainage tubes in to measure how much fluid I was losing. I had to measure the amount of fluid passing through the tubes every two to three hours. I eventually developed something called a seroma. A seroma is a pocket of fluid that keeps coming back. The doctors did not know why the seromas kept coming back. Each time it was more difficult for my doctors to treat because they had to be drained. I had to have different types of IVs and central lines. I had a pic line, which is a line that ran up my arm to the main artery beside my heart. It had two valves. They put me on hypoallipids and TPN (total protein nutrition). I was fed overnight during a twelve-hour period. This gave me all the nutrients necessary to sustain life.

After my initial surgery and in the midst of all my new complications, they started me off with Percodan and other narcotics, like Lortab for pain. Shortly after that, I discovered that I was allergic to aspirin, which is contained in Percodan. I developed hypoglycemia, which is when your glucose levels drop and you begin to suffer symptoms, such as tremors, irritability, sweating, and shaking hands. I was also anemic, which is low iron levels in the blood. I also developed a chronic low white blood count, which meant that I had to be very careful of what I came in contact with because my white blood cells were unable to defend against germs. Asthma and numerous allergies followed. The last eight years were very frustrating, not knowing if a regular doctor visit would end with me being admitted into the hospital due to some new complication.

I could not handle all the surgeries; the medications affected my body: hernias, obstructions of my bowel, lesions, adhesions, and blockages in my colon. All of this was going on inside my body, and on top of that, I was in two car accidents. While all of this was going on inside my body, the pain elevated to an all-time high. I was now in and out of the hospital all the time, which began to take a toll on me mentally and physically. It got to the point where I was in the hospital for thirty days to ninety days at a time. I started to develop an ileus, which is a pocket of gas in the colon that will not move. It is extremely painful. Over the past eleven years, I have had ten to fifteen of these as a result of all the surgeries. Finally, my doctors made the decision to call in a new set of specialists for assistance. By 1999, I had had a total of thirty surgeries.

I required home health care. I was introduced to the world of home health agencies. My experiences with the agencies were not good. When they came to my home, I felt as though they were trying to control me instead of helping me. I was already fighting for my life, and I did not need the added stress that came along with the home health-care agencies. I tried several different agencies. I fired almost every agency available in the Richmond area.

This was a very difficult time for me. Eventually, I was able to find an agency that I was comfortable with. They taught my family how to properly care for me. My parents were my primary caregivers. After my niece, Crystal, graduated from high school, she came to live with my husband and me because she was attending college near where we lived. She then became my sole caregiver. A CNA, certified nursing assistant, attended to my hygiene, meal preparation, and medication management. I also received physical therapy and occupational therapy. I was too weak to stand or walk by myself.

Due to me being on Percocet, which is very hard on the liver, it was challenging for my doctors to keep me hydrated. On January 8, 1999, I was admitted into the hospital again, which was about the twentieth time. This time it was for severe stomach pain, vomiting, nausea, and dehydration. My hope of getting better began slipping away. My veins became cystic or hard. I could not have an IV inserted, so they put in a PICC line. This was used to give me IV medications and to take blood work. Over the next eleven years, I had nine PICC lines. A PICC line is not intended to be in the body more than three months at a time because it can cause infection. That is exactly what happened to me next. I got my first staph infection. At this time, I was out of the hospital, so I went to my doctor because I was running a very high fever. He sent me to St. Mary's Hospital. They ran several tests and had a doctor from the Centers for Disease Control and Prevention come to assess the situation. This infection contaminated my entire bloodstream. I ended up spending two months in the hospital while on the antibiotic Vicomycin to treat the infection. I was still in chronic pain and nauseated all the time. During this hospital stay, I also developed bedsores.

In January 2000, I was admitted into the hospital again for the removal of an abscess and blockage in my colon. This was the first time that I had a bone marrow test. During this test, a hole is drilled in your lower back, and bone marrow is drawn out to be tested for cancer. It is a very painful test.

The second type of central line that I received was a port-a-cath. A port-a-cath is a device that is surgically implanted in your right or left side of your chest. It is about the size of your thumbnail. A needle is placed inside the port-a-cath. A port-a-cath is more durable than a PICC line. I can remember it like yesterday when I had my first port-a-cath inserted. The pain was excruciating, and I remember asking the nurses if it was supposed to be that painful. I was told that the pain should go away in a couple of days.

The pain did not go away in a couple of days. I remember coming home with my set of home health nurses. They were really nice. I named them my dream team. I received a new needle while I was asleep one day. I didn't feel when my nurse put the first needle in, but when she put the second needle in, I remember it very well. When she put the needle in, puss flew everywhere. My doctor told me to get to the hospital immediately. This was Christmas Eve.

When I got there, a whole tube of fluid was removed from the site where my portacath was. I was hysterical when I was told that I had to go into an emergency surgery to have the portacath removed. My system was infected and septic again. I had a fever of 104 degrees. I was given one of the strongest antibiotics to fight this infection. I remained in the hospital for ten days. My home health nurses had to pack the wound twice daily for about two months.

Following the infection, I did my best to care for myself. My system would no longer tolerate tap water. I had to switch to bottled water. I learned a lot about my body throughout these complications. The most important thing that I learned was to appreciate my body and what it means to have good health. Too bad for me, it was a little too late. That's what I thought at the time, but now I feel that as long as you live, it is never too late. You can always make a change.

Shortly after this ordeal, I was hospitalized again. This time it was for chronic diarrhea, constipation, and pain. I was on pain medication at the time, and my doctor would say to me, "Lynette, I don't want to see you get addicted to this medication. I would hate to see that happen to you." I told him that would not happen to me. Well, because of everything that I was going through, such as the pain, not being able to eat, infection, anemia, chronic low white blood count, etc., my body became addicted. The fact that my body was atypical played a major part in this.

With this condition, my blood work would never show that I had a big infection. I still run a low white chronic blood count, and to this day, the doctors are unable to explain why that happens.

Also during this time, I had to have blood transfusions. I am O positive, which means I am a universal donor. So anyone can use my blood, however only O positive blood can combine with O positive blood. So I was told I needed a blood transfusion because my red blood cell count had dropped down to six, whereas the average blood count is anywhere from twelve to eighteen, depending on the person. I also had a vitamin deficiency. I was not getting an adequate supply of iron and other vital nutrients, which contributed to my low blood count.

Everyone in my immediate family got tested to try to find a possible donor for me. It turned out that both my parents were O positive; however, since my father had a history of cancer, that canceled him out. My mom has diabetes and she opted to not be a donor. My nephew was also O positive, but he was unable to arrive within the time frame that I needed the blood, so I received blood from the blood bank. Just having a blood transfusion in itself is very risky and life threatening. The biggest risk is having a negative reaction to the blood, which could instantly kill you. After having a blood transfusion, the first fifteen to thirty minutes afterward are critical. This is the time period in which if you are going to have a reaction, you will have it. So, after my transfusion I was extremely nervous not knowing whether or not I was going to react negatively. Since I had been at St. Mary's Hospital so often, everyone there knew me, and after my transfusion, the nurses were all keeping a close eye on me, which helped ease my tension. This was my first transfusion, which was in 1999, and since then I have about eight to ten transfusions. The blood transfusion helped some, but it still was not enough. I was referred to a hematologist and gastrointestinal specialist. They put me on a medication called Procrit, which helps to boost the red blood count. With me being atypical, it took many years for my blood to stabilize. Every month I had to get a B12 injection. Just recently, I was able to stop getting that shot, and I haven't had a Procrit shot in ten to eleven months. Up to the year 2004, I was getting these shots once a month.

I go to the Virginia Cancer Institute every other week to have them check my CBC (complete blood count). They also gave me a CMP (complete metabolic panel), which gives you all of your electrolytes, like chloride, potassium, iron, and sodium. Because I was malnourished, I was always potassium depleted. Potassium is a key electrolyte because the heart functions on a potassium pump. I was sent home again with an IV and a bag. There are three types of IV bags that can be administered. The first is a saline bag to keep you hydrated, the second is a bag with potassium in it, and the third is a bag with lactated ringers. Lactated ringers help the cells. I was on these for about seven to eight months. When all of this was going on, I was taking about fourteen to sixteen

Percocets per day to help deal with the chronic pain, on top of about twenty other medications I was taking each day. Most of it was for pain; some was for the nausea and the vomiting.

My life now consisted of survival, living from day to day, minute to minute. I can remember days when I would sit downstairs in my recliner, and I would ask God, "God, please, please, please just give me one minute of reprieve from the pain, just thirty seconds of reprieve from the pain," and I didn't get that. There also was a time when I realized that my life was totally dependent on others because I was no longer able to take care of myself. And I'd been taking care of myself for as long as I can remember—including being a teenager and not only taking care of myself but taking care of my parents and other family members. And that was a huge burden on me. But there was nothing I could do about it. I was helpless.

And the really sad part was that every time I looked at my husband, all I saw was sadness because this was his wife, and there was nothing he could do for me. He felt totally helpless because he could do nothing but see his wife suffer.

I say now that if I didn't have God going into the surgery, then I would not be writing this book today. Like many people before me, I could have died, but I didn't. I suffered a lot. I suffered being in the hospital ten to ninety days at time and being away from my daughter and husband. "Rough, rough, rough, really rough," as the Chapman wrote in my medical notes. I want everyone to know that when you are in the hospital, the nurses just don't ask you questions for no reason. They ask those questions to put it into your medical records. They notice when you don't have family members come in to see you. When they ask you questions like, "Is anyone coming to see you today?" they are not just asking; they are asking so that they can put it in your medical records. When the Chapman came up to visit me one day, she wrote in my medical records, "I have never met anyone in my entire life that has such faith in God, in spite of what she is going through. I don't know if I could be as strong as she is, and she is such a positive person." When I read that, I began to cry because I didn't remember that visit from her. She also said, "Prayer is an important spiritual resource to the patient. Patient family present and very supportive."

Some of the medication that I was taking, other than Percocet, was Ambien. Ambien is a sedative that helps with sleep. I was taking that, and I was taking Promethazine, which is a nausea medication. I was also taking Pepcid AC for acid reflux.

Since 1999, some of the notes I've read about my experiences in the hospital say chronic pain, right lower quadrant, poor IV access, etc., so they put in a central line.

A central line is an IV access that goes into your neck, either the right or left side. It is called an internal jugular CDP line with triple luminum. This line had three ports through which they could feed me the TPN. They could give me a blood transfusion, and they could also take blood. That's what the triple luminum means. A central line is not meant to stay in for a long period of time. The longest you should have one in is about ten days. I got an infection from one of those too. I went back to the hospital and was put back on Vicomycin and other IV antibiotics. It says that I had chronic pain, diarrhea, constipation, hypoglycemia, malabsorption, and rum-seroma, which was a pocket of fluid that kept coming back.

So in 1999, I was in the hospital thirty-two days. I wasn't able to walk so I had to have extensive physical therapy and occupational therapy. I had no energy whatsoever. I was a sick—really sick—person. The only thing that I hadn't done was die, and I made it through that year also, but my health continued to decline. At the end of 1999, because I was taking so much pain medication, including the Tylenol and Percocet, I had to come off that and they had to put me on methadone. I only associated methadone with being a medication to help heroin addicts to come off heroin. So when they said that to me, I told them no because I was not a heroin addict, and I didn't need to be on methadone.

One of my doctors, my gastrointestinal specialist, who I am very close to because he has been my physician since day one, had a meeting with my husband and me in my hospital room. Leon and I were adamant about me not being put on methadone. After Dr. G thoroughly explained how methadone would be used in my situation, I asked him to step out for a minute so that I could discuss it with my husband and come up with a final decision. Evidently, he heard us fussing, so he entered back into the room. He called my husband Ty. He said, "Ty, I'm going to tell you something. This is not the time for you and Lynette to be arguing with one another, and she is going to need more than she ever has before." He acknowledged that he had overstepped his boundaries by coming back into the room, but he made it known that I really needed to come off Percocet because of the negative way that it was affecting my body and how methadone would help me.

I started on methadone. I started out taking five milligrams a day. Of course, my tolerance was high so that was nothing for me. After about three to four days, my dose was increased to ten milligrams a day, and that still didn't do anything for me. So they increased it up to fifteen. That still didn't do anything, so they increased it to twenty milligrams, along with another painkiller that wasn't as strong. Finally, I began to get some relief, but it made me like a zombie.

Over the next five years, things began to deteriorate even more. I had to have emergency surgery to remove another hernia. I was placed in the intensive care unit. As a result of my obesity, I developed a heart murmur. This was from years of my heart working overtime. I lost my vision to the point where I could only see black and blue, and it happened so quickly. I'll never forget when it happened. I was watching TV with my niece and said to her, "Crystal, did the TV screen seem like the light in it went down or something?" She said, "No, Aunt Lynn." I told her that I could only see black and blue. What was happening was that I was so severely dehydrated that it affected my vision. I had to go in the hospital, and they had to insert a feeding tube into my stomach, which was called a PEG tube. I was being fed Jevity through the PEG tube. This was in the year 2000.

When the nurse would come and hook me up and stuff like that, we could actually see my stomach expand. It was such excruciating pain. When they went inside, my insides were totally messed up from organs being moved around and operated on so much. My surgery was only supposed to last one hour, but it ended up being six hours. I also ended up back in intensive care with a blood transfusion because my hemoglobin dropped while I was on the operating table. I think it was at a nine and it dropped to a six, so they had to hurry up and give me a blood transfusion. Then I developed something called an arrhythmia. This is a heart condition that is typically prevalent in older people between the ages of seventy and eighty. Due to this, I had to go through a whole series of stress tests for my heart to see if there was any permanent damage. The test required that I walk on a treadmill. Being that I couldn't walk alone and even with help I was unstable, they injected something into my veins that made me feel like I was having a heart attack. The feeling did not last any longer than about thirty seconds, but that thirty seconds seemed like forever. The test came back good, and I had about four more tests done with the cardiologist. I guess it was 2000 when I lost my vision, and I also realized that the painkillers were a major problem.

I have always been sharp and very smart. When you take painkillers, this slows your mental process down, and my mind is my most prized asset. It really slowed it down. I was like a zombie and a junky. My husband would come home and I would be knocked out asleep, and there are a lot of things that I don't remember that people are telling me that they remember.

Due to all of the things that had happened to me, I was in therapy for many years. In 1999 when I was in the hospital, I was first introduced to an antidepressant, Xanax. I was so depressed that my surgeon suggested that I talk to someone, so he did a referral for a psychiatrist to come and talk to me. Xanax really didn't help my mood; it just helped me not to be so anxious. It helped with the anxiety, but that didn't last long either. I had to go on other antidepressants. I can remember one day I was referred to a psychologist that I used to go and talk to three times a week. Not only was I dealing with my life, but I was also dealing with issues with my mom and dad, which didn't make things any better; it made things worse. Being able to talk to someone who is neutral and on the outside looking in helped a great deal. I continued talking with this psychologist for many years. I had to stop going to therapy to deal with what was happening in my life. It's like one day the life that I wanted to live was totally gone. It was taken away from me for years.

It was 2007 and this was only my second Christmas spent at home in the past eleven years. I spent every holiday, every birthday—my husband's and my daughter's—in the hospital. This was one of the main reasons that I was severely depressed. I had to go to rehabilitation to learn how to read and to talk all over again. I had to use all these things: a rolator, a walker, and bedside commode. I would think, *Lord I just can't take this. I just can't take this. Lord, I'm doing everything I can do to keep my sanity, and it is just not working. Lord, help me, help me, help me.* I begged to God for so many years. There were years that I couldn't do anything but say, "Jesus." I know that he only answers the prayers of the righteous and those were what had gotten me through. I couldn't even pray for myself at certain points because I was so overtaken by depression. Depression is something that I would not wish on anyone—not even my worst enemy.

As you know, I had the gastric bypass in 1997. I was referring back to my journal and my medical records, and I even have a tape were I recorded one of my home health nurses back in 2004. Not only had I had forty surgeries, I don't know some of the things that happened over the course of the last eleven years. If it was not for my journal, I would not have any type of recollection of certain things. I was on two different types of pain medications at the same time. I was on, methadone, and the Fentanyl patch. All of those are addicting narcotics. I thought that I was off the Percocet, but evidently they gave me the Percocet during the interim years of 1999 to 2004. I think that because I had so much going on and I had been in the hospital so many times, and the pain was just unreal to deal with, and I know they were giving me two different types of pain medication in my IV, but I didn't know that I came home on those medications. But I did.

I never thought that the gastric bypass was a quick fix like most people. Some people think that it is a quick way to lose weight. I went through so many difficulties that I never had the pleasure of thinking that way. I lost the weight, but I was never able to enjoy it. I didn't have the physical ability to shop for smaller clothes. Before I had the surgery, I wore a size thirty-two dress. When I was big, I was never able to buy things from Lane Bryant or any other popular plus-size women's store because they only carried up to size 28. I had to shop at a specialty store in which the clothing was very expensive.

The purpose of me sharing my experience about this surgery is to make people aware of the complications that can arise if you find yourself on the extreme end of a medical procedure. This book is also to educate people on how to become advocates for themselves. I want people to ask questions about anything that they do not fully understand. Especially ask questions about complications that can arise in extreme cases. It is okay to be inquisitive about your health. Sometimes doctors may use terminology that you may not understand. Let the doctor know that he needs to speak in a language for the layperson. Don't be afraid to ask questions. Remember that you are your own best advocate. If your doctor is unwilling to explain things to you in way that you understand, seek another doctor. After all, you only get one you. It's your job to be responsible for your own well-being.

I must say that, all in all, I have been truly blessed to have good doctors with wonderful bedside manners. They have gone through everything with me. They have watched my daughter grow from a little girl into the beautiful young lady that she is today. I have been truly blessed. Not too many people can say that they have good doctors and good specialists. My doctors took every step of the journey with me. They were there for me emotionally through the good, the bad, and the ugly.

I hope that in reading and hearing my story parents will give more attention to the eating habits of their children. I hope parents will teach and implement the values of healthy living as readily as they would teach their children to read and write. The quality of life for the child will depend greatly on the parents' regard for instilling values for a healthy lifestyle. Once these values are internalized as a child, hopefully the child will continue to make lifestyle decisions based on those values. This greatly decreases the likelihood of making poor choices concerning food, drugs, or alcohol, which are major areas of concern for young people today. As I mentioned earlier, when I was a child, we ate what was put in front of us. We had to clean our plates. We ate what our parents could afford. My parents thought this was how you raised a healthy child. Today, most parents have been exposed to the "food groups." Healthy living is constantly being advertised on TV. There really is no excuse.

If parents implement healthy living as a part of the child's everyday experiences, the odds of the child having to go through this type of surgery as an adult and being faced with life-threatening decisions, or even being told that they may not survive, would be significantly lower. What parent would not want to give his or her child the best possible odds for having a good life?

Many people ask if I could go back, would I have the surgery? My answer is somewhat complicated: yes and no. Yes, because my faith in God was made stronger through my trials. No, because of all the things I know today about those types of surgeries. Very few people who have had the gastric bypass, with complications similar to mine, have lived to tell their story. I did so. I tell my story so that no little girl or boy will have to go through childhood, teenage years, or even adulthood suffering from complications due to obesity. My goal is to educate parents. It doesn't have to be that way, even if you are suffering from obesity. You, the parent, have the ability to stop the cycle. I gave my child the nutritional values that I have learned the hard way. She can now pass it on to her children and them to their children. This is the only way that we as a nation can fight obesity and many of the other things that plague our youth.

CHAPTER 7

Depression

*A*lthough *I touched a little on* me being depressed in the previous chapter, I feel that it is important for me to go a little deeper just in case someone may be going through the same thing and may need some reassurance. I realized that I was depressed when I wasn't getting better. I was getting worse. I always thought that I would get better, but it wasn't happening soon enough. I believe that depression first started to set in when I was admitted in the hospital in 1998 for the Gastric Bypass revision. Anyone that has ever been depressed knows that it is such a horrible feeling. It's like you have no hope; you're always crying and you're always sad.

I am typically a very social person. However, I withdrew from people. I didn't want to talk to anybody anymore. I only spoke if I was questioned. My surgeon, because he knew me so well said, "Lynette I think you need to talk to someone." He did a consult for me to talk to a psychiatrist while I was in the hospital. The psychiatrist asked about my family history. I told him about my sister having some mental challenging. The psychiatrist didn't have to question too much with me as to why I was depressed, he simply read my medical records. He asked me if I thought that I would get better. I told him, "I don't know." I was constantly introduced to new medications to help my condition.

I was put on my first antidepressant in 1998, Xanax. I started out with the minimum dose that is recommended which is 0.5 milligrams three times a day. I was told that it could take while before I would see any results. I was on Xanax for a period of time but the Xanax did not work for me. I was then prescribed another antidepressant to help lift my moods which was Effexor. Effexor made me even more depressed. They had to stop the effects of it. I was introduced to Ambien, which is a sedative to with sleep. Since I wasn't sleeping due to the chronic pain, I was given even more pain killers. Still, it was not working for me.

I was such a challenge for my doctors early on after the surgery. **I was told that they had never seen anyone to with as many complications.**

They had patients who had complications, but none to this extreme. Not only were they frustrated but I was frustrated also. After being on an antidepressant for a while, my mood lifted some. Depression is like being in a deep, deep hole; a hole so big that you can't dig your way out. All you want is for the next day to come. When the next day comes you still wake up feeling absolutely hopeless again. There was no hope, at least that's what I felt. I felt hopeless, like I was going to die. I often wondered, "Am I going to leave my husband and my child?" It was a really, really rough time in my life. I saw a psychologist up to 3 times a week. He would just sit there while I poured my heart out. He would give me suggestions at times. I've been so blessed to have such a wonderful team of doctors. I remember my first psychologist, Doctor N. She was so special to me. I told her things that my husband wanted me to tell him, but I couldn't because he was already so worried about me. He had never seen me like this. I was always such a lively person. It just seemed as if my spirit had just been taken away. However, I can say I never, ever contemplated suicide. Taking my own life was never an option. Were there days that I didn't want to live? Yes. Were there days I could have easily overdosed on medications? Yes. I didn't. I never contemplated doing that. I remember talking to Doctor N. I talked about disagreeing with my doctors on some things. She would say, "Lynette you are such a fighter, you will overcome this." I said to Dr. N, "I can't see that, I can't see coming out of this hole." She said, "You will, you will." Then we would set up another appointment.

My best friend, Brenda Simmons called me to make sure I had a ride to my appointments since my husband had to work during the day. She also would pick Tiffany up in the mornings; take her to and from school. When she brought Tiffany home in the evenings she would sit and talk to me and encourage me. She also was that friend that would call me the day before to make sure that I would keep my appointment. I didn't particularly want to go back to see the psychologist, but she would literally call every morning that I had an appointment and say ,"Girl get out the bed." I would be like, "Brenda I don't feel like going," and she would say "Get out the bed Lynn, James (which is her husband) is going to take you to your appointment and I will see you in the evening when I bring Tiffany home." She is the one friend that stuck with me through everything. She would sense when I was having a bad day. I would always try to not show it around Tiffany.

When Tiffany would come in from school I would always ask "How was your day stink (stink is Tiffany's nickname that I gave her)?" "How was your day at school today?" "Do you have any homework?" She would say, yes or no. She would then go in her room with Mya, Brenda's daughter, which is my god daughter.

This part of my life was very traumatic. It finally set in that I wasn't getting better, I was getting worse. It hit close to home when I was unable to drive or to do anything for myself. I was totally dependent on others for every single thing: to help me get out of bed, to take a bath, to put in my feeding tube. I went through a whole series of feeding tubes. They couldn't put a feeding tube in my stomach because I had so much scar tissue, so they put the tube down my nose. It just so happened that I was allergic to the plastic on the tube and it started to affect my frontal lobe. The tube caused chronic sinus pain and headaches as allergic reactions. I had the tube in for a month. No one should be subjected to the things that I have gone through in the last eleven years of my life. I know that people go through hard times, but I think no one will ever really know what I've been through from simply hearing and hearing my story, except for my family and close friends, which are very few. A couple of my close friends are no longer there because they couldn't weather the storm. There are only a couple of close friends of ours that really stayed in our lives. Everyone else abandoned us.

The Gastric Bypass was a surgery to improve my quality of life, but I ended up with no quality of life. My life of independence was gone. How do you handle something like that? Some people commit suicide, people give up and some people just give in to death. However, for me there was always this little ray of hope deep down inside. It wouldn't let me give up. A lot of that came from my husband. He wouldn't let me give up. He knew I wanted to, but he wouldn't let me. He would call me all through the day. He would miss work to stay home with me. He knew he had to work because there was no one to help take care of our family. No one was willing to help us. My parents had been around the first few years but they had their own lives and had to provide for themselves. My husband's side of the family had no interactions with us at all. How do you deal with it? Well the only way I knew how to deal with it was through the help of God. Looking back now, I know that if I didn't have God when I went into this surgery in 1997, then I wouldn't be telling this story. I did have God and put all of my trust in him. I questioned him many days, "Why lord, why lord why, why me. I honor you word, I treat people right, and I give when you say to give." Many theologians say to never question God. Put in a situation like I was, I've learned to never say what you will never do. Sometimes

you will do things that you said you would never do....
and I did. I promised my parents that I would never
do drugs. However, surgeries left me in chronic pain
and I found myself taking massive doses of narcotics
just to deal with the pain.

CHAPTER 8

Prescription Drug Addiction/Detox

I thought my life was over. I took pills to wake up and pills to go to bed. I was sleeping all day and I had no energy. The pills had become my means of existing from day to day. However, the hypocritical thing about it all was that they were also slowly killing me. I had become an addict. Not only were the pills killing me physically but they were also killing me socially, emotionally and spiritually. I did not exist anymore. It was hard for me to even remember who I use to be. Do you know what that's like? Do you know what it feels like to wake up one day and be gone mentally? I guess it would be similar to having an out of body experience. Some people claim to have had them in times of near death experiences. From what I've read this usually is an isolated incident and feeling. Almost like a dream that you just woke up from. Well, for me the dream lasted for days, for weeks for months. At times, I doubted that I would ever wake up from it.

In 2002 I knew that I was in trouble but I could not help myself. I was ashamed of what I had allowed to happen. My family saw the signs and tried to warn me that I was becoming irritable, moody, and bothered by anyone who spoke of my medications and all the sleeping that I was doing. They would often ask me if I was taking my medications according to the prescription. I would always say yes, but soon found myself being irritated at the thought of them asking such a question. I would place my medication near my bed, within arm's reach. On some days, I could have sworn that somebody had moved them farther away. Even in my weakened state, I was defensive. I had begun to defend the lifestyle that I had fallen into. For example, I needed pain killers for this ailment and another for another ailment, etc. I could always justify taking the pills with reminding people of all that I had been through. I guess one could say that I set myself up. I was my own worst enemy.

I was approached by my surgeon who was very

concerned about my condition. He insisted that I come off pain medications. As I listened to him that day, I wondered what would become of me. How would I deal with the pain? To say the least, I was afraid, very afraid. This had been my lifestyle for what seemed like forever. How would my body react? He referred me to a pain specialist. I still remember the look on his face at our first visit. Before speaking to me, his eyes moved slowly from one side of my hospital room to the other. There was so much to take in. At that time I was hooked up to an IV. I had a pump for this and something else for that. I was hooked up all over the place. The look on his face was what appeared to be utter disbelief. I tried not to show it, but it bothered me because I felt like he was judging me. I was made up in my mind to just do what I had to do and not let shame keep me from moving forward. As he left my room that day, he rode the elevator down to the first floor with my niece Crystal. Crystal later told me that he had thought that she was my daughter. He told her that he had never seen anyone with the problems that he had witnessed in meeting me that day. Needless to say, he never returned. It wasn't until 2006 before I saw him again.

My faith was truly tested because I had to make the decision whether to come off the opiates or continue with no quality of life. At this point I was taking 16 Methadone's per day with about 20 other medications I was taking for other health issues. My faith won the battle as my decision was to trust God with my life. I thought of all the times that I had tried to work it out myself by medicating and over medicating. It was now time for me to step aside. Faith was the only thing that I had left. My pride, self-esteem, confidence any everything else was little to none at that time. What else could I lose, my life? As I thought about this, it was clear that my life was not life at all. I had only been existing. Certainly God had much more for me than to just exist. Then like a ray of light shining through a dark cloud, I remembered something from my favorite book. It was simply this: "He came that I might have life and have it more abundantly."

Things weren't exactly smooth sailing after that. If you have ever experienced detox, you know that your very own body will attempt to betray you. I felt that I was in a war within myself mentally. Physically, I was done. You could have stuck a fork in me. It was an all up hill battle. Every issue that you can imagine brought more complications to my detox program. The very medications that are commonly used in cases like mines, were not advisable due to possible complications with my heart. I thought, "Oh God, what's next, this is so much to bare." In the far corners of my mind, I envisioned what this news would mean to my family. Here was another setback. What could I do? That's when my faith kicked into action again. I said to myself, "This is an uphill battle and I am too tired to climb." At that moment a verse from an old familiar song came to mind, "The battle is not yours, it's the Lord's." Detoxing was one of the hardest things that I have ever had to do. Coming off opiates is somewhat inhumane. The body goes through so much trauma. You can't eat or drink and 90% of the time all you do is regurgitate. My body was fighting me all the way. It's similar to a heavy smoker being suddenly told that there are no more cigarettes and that cigarettes don't exist anymore .What do you think is going to happen in just a matter of time? Well, I'll tell you, somebody is going to lose it big time and in a bad way. That's exactly what the body does. It goes slam off. It was a most miserable experience.

After the hospital stay the next phase was to have a pellet implanted in my stomach. It was called a Naltrexone implant. This was supposed to block the receptor that causes you to the crave the opiates. Well, that did not happen to me. It was so difficult. I could not eat or drink and had no energy until the third week. My doctor told me to go the emergency room. I was told that I had viral bronchitis. I was given something for pain and nausea. The pellet most of the time has to be repeated at least 2 times. However, I never knew when the pellet wore off. I was free for the first time in a long time! I remember what God had said in my spirit. He had told me to trust him ...and I did.

CHAPTER 9

Overcoming Life Obstacles

*A*s *I look over my life,* I have been dealing with obstacles all my life. The Enemy has been trying kill me, even as a little girl when I took an overdose of my father's sleeping pills. When you have so msany obstacles in your life, there are two things you can do. You can have a positive attitude or a negative attitude. The positive attitude will help you to deal with the obstacles that you are facing. A negative attitude will make people not want to be around you, and it isolates you from family and friends.

The obstacles that God allows us to go through are to test our faith. We often say I would do anything for God, but let's be realistic: no one wants to suffer in pain all the time. This fifteen-year journey is something I would have never thought would happen to me.

I can remember on day when I was in the hospital and actually begging God to just get rid of the pain and then I would be a soldier for him the rest of my life. He knew I was not ready for that assignment yet, so he continued to let things happen to me. When I started writing this book in 1999, I think I had already had about twenty surgeries due to the complications of the gastric bypass. My life was totally out of control, and so was I. I thought, *Why, God, are you allowing all these bad things happen to me?* I thought I was doing everything he wanted me to do: paying my tithes and offering, praying for those that had mistreated me. What was happening to me just did not make any sense until about three years later, after I had an additional ten surgeries. The hospital became my permanent home. When I was in the hospital, I had to become a human filter. What I mean by that is I had to learn the terminology that the nurses and doctors were saying when it came to me.

Here I am thirteen years later, September 2012, and finally finishing up my book, which is an assignment from God. I have been through so many more things that I will have to write another book to go into further detail. Just to name a few things, I continue to suffer from being anemic, having hypoglycemia and chronic low blood count, and not knowing how my days will go until they actually come. I have had about six more surgeries, including a total right-knee replacement, numerous hernias removed, portacath insertions, and my most recent surgery, which was to have my colon removed because it stopped working. I came extremely close to death during this surgery. I was not having bowel movements for two weeks at a time. It got to the point that the pain was unbearable. So I have to make another critical decision. When the doctors opened me up, they told my husband and daughter that they did not know how I was still alive because of all the toxins that were built up in my body because they could not be released. I also was losing an unknown amount of blood, which required two emergency blood transfusions. I complained that my neck was hurting where the central line was. After performing a Doppler, the doctors learned that I had a blood clot in my neck from the line not being properly inserted.

There is a lot more to my story, but I feel that my mission has been accomplished thus far. If God lays upon me to continue with this, I will do so and continue to share my ongoing story in hopes of providing courage, support, and knowledge to those who may need it.   Be Blessed!